Ultimate Sugar-free Desserts

50+ Decadent Recipes

HARSH KEDIA

First published 2022 by Pan
an imprint of Pan Macmillan Publishing India Private Limited
707, Kailash Building, 26 K. G. Marg, New – 110 001
www.panmacmillan.co.in

Pan Macmillan, The Smithson, 6 Briset St. Farringdon, London EC1M 5NR
Associated companies throughout the world
www.panmacmillan.com

ISBN 978-93-90742-27-1

Photography by Alok Verma

1 3 5 7 9 8 6 4 2

Designed by Haitenlo Semy
Printed and bound in India by Replika Press Pvt. Ltd.

For my parents

A
DIABET
CHE

Contents

Foreword

For me, baking was always like entering a world of mystery. I've always been fascinated by simple ingredients coming together to create big magic. As a young girl, I experimented in my home kitchen for fun, using instincts and my taste buds as guiding forces. As I grew older, I learnt about formulas and ratios, and the precise and scientific nature of baking. It was pure maths and chemistry. Years later, culinary school taught me to respect each ingredient. I would look at recipes and ask myself, 'why does this ingredient belong here?'

Sugar is obviously an essential and crucial ingredient in baking – not only does it add sweetness, but it helps with structure and adds moisture to the baked good as well. Baking without sugar is one of the most challenging things to do in a pastry kitchen.

A few years ago, I gave up processed sugar for six months while training for the half-marathon in Mumbai. As someone with a sweet tooth, this exercise was pure torture. I can't even begin to imagine what it must be like to go through one's entire adult life knowing consuming sugar is lethal for one's health. Especially, if they are like me and love having desserts!

I met Harsh a few years ago when he joined the marketing team at Le15 Patisserie. I always found him to be quick-witted, creative and someone who had big dreams. He'd tell me stories of his weight loss, of not being able to live a somewhat normal life where his food and diet were concerned and how he'd always be the person who carried his own cake to parties.

It makes me pleased to see the progress he's made in his career since. Being an entrepreneur requires one to wear many hats at work and he's managed to shuffle between running the business and working in the kitchen. It's impressive what he's achieved in a short span of time.

I'm sure this book will be a handy bible to all those readers, like Harsh, who've found it difficult to bake without sugar. The range of recipes is vast and varied, and there's something for everyone. My father is diabetic, and I often make sugar-free desserts for him. So, I can't wait to use the recipes from this book in my home.

Baking something from scratch is a wonderful feeling and I hope the readers find the magic in the kitchen, even if you have to leave the sugar out!

All my love,
POOJA DHINGRA

Introduction

As Indians, we are born with a natural sweet tooth and being diagnosed with diabetes leads one to think that the diagnosis is the end of all of that. But that does not need to be the case. This book shall be the knight in shining armour for your sweet tooth!

The story of this book starts when I was eight years old. I would sneak into the kitchen to imitate the dishes my mom made for me. Fifteen years since I first wandered into the kitchen, my passion for playing with flavours has only grown and manifested into a life and career I deeply cherish in my life. Nothing has ever veered me away from spending all my time in the kitchen. Not my parents who cautiously watched over me while I was working the stove. Not my friends who would coax me to come play outside. Not even finding out I had diabetes at the age of fifteen. In fact, more than ever, my curiosity peaked then. I would spend the whole day perfecting sugar-free, wholesome recipes. It became my life's goal, as it remains even now. As soon as I received my diagnosis, my diet was controlled with military precision. My sugar intake was limited, and I was deprived of a cake for two of my own birthdays. But a foodie cannot be kept away from their favourite food for long. Accepting my diagnosis and coming to terms with it was a tedious process. Once I had done that, I understood I would have to find a resolution for my dessert cravings on my own. This book is a coming together of that journey – a journey that allowed a foodie to enjoy their favourite foods again without constantly worrying about their sugar levels. It is a product of my long hours in the kitchen, my hard work and my dreams.

While food is mostly a question of supplying nutrition to one's body in the rest of the animal kingdom, humans, and especially Indians, believe food to be far more than merely a source of sustenance. In Indian culture, food occupies a unique space. Every family has its own set of recipes, ingredients and cooking techniques. While the general dish remains the same, each community, region and family has a unique way of preparing it. India has struggled for years to reduce its fussy food aversion to restaurants. While fasting too, Indians remain obsessed with eating. We even 'fast' alongside our elders, as delectable fried delicacies – which are allegedly prepared from ingredients permissible to consume when fasting – are handed out all day. In this case, the 'permissible' foods vary from household to household, resulting in the fasting becoming a big celebration that culminates at night with some more delicious food for the entire family to enjoy. It is also a way for Indians to honour the dead and relish life. Indians are unique in our emotional connection to food, in addition to our technological interaction with food.

The idea of this book subconsciously arose when I was attending a friend's birthday party as a child. The highlight for me, as it is for every kid, was the cake. But because I was a diabetic child, I could not have it. I felt alienated from my friends; in fact, I had never felt more alone. But after that incident, I made a promise to myself that I would create a diabetic-friendly cake one day, which I would then carry with me to every party. That is exactly what I did. This book will ensure that no other kid has to forego the cake-eating experience just because they are living with diabetes. And it also opens up a new world for millions of others who are trying to lead a more sugar-free life.

Key Ingredients

STEVIA

Are you counting calories? Or trying to tone your body? Do you have a diabetic sweet tooth? Or are you by any chance a hardcore vegan or a consumer of organic products? If your answers to any of these questions is yes, then Stevia rebaudiana Bertoni is your friend from now on! Stevia, often recognized as candy or sweet plant, is the one-stop solution to all these struggles in your daily lives. It is family to the sunflower for your organic interests! (Now you know why the sunflower seeds taste so sweet. Genes, you see!) This sweet plant is a non-nutritive sweetener, thus, assuring no calorie count.

Interestingly, stevia is almost 300 times sweeter than the normal table sugar used in the kitchens. This has led to the general estimated measure that 2 tablespoons of stevia are equivalent to a cup of sugar. No ingredient is perfect in every sense, but stevia is closer to fitting your sugar-free requirements. In the research and repeated experiments conducted by food scientists, it was found that stevia had a sour aftertaste, which affected the standard flavour. But, through further studies, this issue was resolved. Among the 150 species of the plant, stevia rebaudiana qualified as a sweetener with negligible to no sour aftertaste.

Previously, stevia had been banned as an additive ingredient by the United States Food and Drug Administration (USFDA), but it could be sold as a dietary supplement. By 2008, however, the ban was taken to bed, and stevia was legalized as a sweetener and not just a supplement after it was declared as GRAS (Generally Recognized As Safe) by the FDA. Even before this, the plant was being sold and remained available in all kinds of garden shops, and people used it in their tea and other beverages. Despite getting the FDA's approval, after this, the plant had to be further purified in order to be used for commercial purposes. And Coca-Cola stepped in. It became the first company to patent its purification method of stevia. Similar steps were carried by other beverage- and agri-related companies like PepsiCo, which used the ingredient, but with different kinds of glycosides like rebaudioside A and stevioside to make their diet and sugar-free soft drinks.

There's a tricky method to consider if you are thinking of getting a stevia plant in your kitchen garden. The raw leaves aren't advisable for direct use, so the steps like harvesting, drying, extracting water and purifying the leaves are a must.

Stevia can be used as a raw ingredient in anything you could think of. Unlike other major artificial sweeteners, stevia can be used for baking as well, whether it be ice cream, chocolates, pies, brownies, cupcakes – you can add it to all for a satisfying, guilt-free experience.

There are certain cooking restrictions, but, with a slight addition, you can fix the balance. For instance, in order to make a bar of chocolate, simply using stevia as an alternative to sugar won't work. The melting properties, plastic viscosity and other such issues have to be taken care of; hence, the combinations of stevia and sugar alcohol like erythritol came into existence. Even so, other competitive elements like inulin and allulose are considered better matches with stevia for making chocolate as they are completely organic and possess better properties.

Stevia is a go-swing solution to all the diabetic sweet dwellers! In fact, it has been found to reduce the risk of pancreatic cancer.

Note: Stevia throughout the book refers to stevia mix/blend which is usually a blend of stevia + erythritol/sugar alcohol readily available in the market. The official body responsible for food security in India (FSSAI) permits only 6% total of stevia leaves/extracts in any packaged 'stevia powder' blend; the rest is usually erythritol.*

ERYTHRITOL

Erythritol is a derived natural sweetener or, in other words, a healthier replacement of sugar in the form of a sugar alcohol or polyols. It can be made from corn using enzymes and fermentation. The fermentation of glucose leads to the production of polyols. Chemist John Stenhouse had first discovered erythritol in 1848, when he found that it is soluble in water and in alcohol. As it is endothermic in nature, it tends to leave a cooling sensation in the mouth, meaning the erythritol soaks in the heat from its surroundings when it is being dissolved in any liquids; although, according to research, once dissolved, it doesn't leave any cooling sensation. Erythritol is known to be a rather young table sweetener.

It is not a food additive, so it is safe to consume it. Erythritol was approved by the FDA as a sugar substitute in 2001, even receiving a GRAS certification in 2001. In 2003, the European Union (EU) and Scientific Committee on Food (SCF) released an opinion stating that erythritol is safe for consumption. Erythritol is largely absorbed in the bloodstream. It is not digested by the body; approximately 90 per cent of it is flushed out of the body via urine without increasing the blood sugar level or the insulin. Erythritol has 0.24 per cent calories per gram, whereas table sugar has 4 calories per gram. It is non-glycaemic, non-cancerous in nature. Of late, erythritol has gained popularity for being keto- and diabetic-friendly. People who follow vegetarian diets, vegan diets, paleo diets and gluten-free diets can safely consume erythritol. However, the sweetness of erythritol when compared to sugar is not 1:1.

When compared to sugar, erythritol is only 70 per cent as sweet as sugar. This makes using it as a sugar substitute a slightly different method. For example, if a recipe calls for 1 cup of sugar, you may want to increase erythritol by 1⅓ cup. But increasing the quantity of erythritol will lead to the baked products becoming less moist and dry. To compensate for the less sweetness, erythritol is blended with other natural sweeteners that have a low glycaemic index, such as stevia, monk fruit and sucralose. These sweeteners are also known as High-Intensity Sweeteners (HIS). Erythritol is the predominant ingredient in all major blends in the market. The ratio of these blends can be anywhere from 200:1 to 2000:1 (1 being High-Intensity Sweetener and 200 or 2000 being erythritol). The key role of erythritol is to mask the flavour of HISs, i.e., to cover any flavours which are not sweet or have any peculiar aftertaste. Erythritol helps to make the product easy to pour and gather in a spoon.

At present, around 95 per cent of the world's erythritol is produced in China with GMO-free corn. Erythritol has a history of being safely used in products, including in beverages, since 1990 after 169 products were authorized for use in foods in many countries, such as Japan, the US, Canada, Brazil, Argentina, Paraguay, Uruguay, China, India, Israel, Mexico, the Philippines, Singapore, Australia, New Zealand, Japan, Korea, Taiwan and Thailand.

Now, can you say yes to yummy desserts?

Note: Erythritol can be substituted for stevia throughout the recipes in this book in the ratio of 1:1. As several recipes in the book include all-purpose flour (simply because certain desserts cannot be prepared without gluten), it will be prudent for all readers to ensure you and your loved ones are enjoying these treats in measured quantities and, thus, staying healthy!

Desi Desserts

Shahi Tukda
Dry Fruit Laddoo
Makhana Kheer
Coconut Barfi
Fruit Kheer
Shrikhand
Sandesh
Mava Cupcakes
Rasgulla
Rasmalai
Gajar ka Halwa
Besan Laddoo
Shahi Falooda

Shahi Tukda

Literally meaning a 'royal piece', shahi tukda is a Mughlai delicacy with deep roots in the city of Hyderabad. This version of the royal delicacy satisfies your sweet tooth without using any sugar or being deep fried. A quick, go-to recipe when you want to impress guests who can't indulge in sweets!

INGREDIENTS

2 slices multigrain bread
50 gms butter
250 ml milk
1 tbsp stevia
100 gms khoya/mava
5–6 almonds
rose petals, for garnishing

METHOD

1. In a bowl, melt the butter.
2. Cut the slices of bread neatly into triangular pieces and spread the butter on both sides.
3. Place the bread slices in the air fryer and fry them for 3–4 minutes at 200°C until they are dark golden brown in colour.

Milk Soak Mixture Recipe

1. In a saucepan, add mava, stevia and milk, and bring the mixture to a boil over medium-high heat.
2. Keep stirring continuously to avoid the mixture from sticking to the bottom of the pan.
3. Reduce the mixture until it is half of the original quantity. Then turn off the heat.
4. Arrange the bread slices on a shallow plate, dip the bread in the milk soak mixture and top the dish using dry fruits of your choice. (I like to include almonds, pistachios and rose petals.)

Dry Fruit Laddoo

I have always enjoyed Indian sweets that are prepared using dry fruits, such as cashew barfi or dry fruit barfi. I still remember my childhood days when my mother would make these for an event at home and I would sneak into the kitchen to grab a couple of them in my hands and one in my mouth!

INGREDIENTS

1 cup almonds
2 cup cashews
1 cup raisins
poppy seeds, as required
½ cup ghee
½ cup pistachios
½ cup walnuts
1 cup raw peanuts
1½ cup dried dates
1 cup oats
1 cup coconut pieces
2 tsp stevia

METHOD

1. Place a pan over medium flame and, once it's hot enough, dry roast walnuts, pistachios, coconut slices, peanuts, raisins, cashews and dried dates for a few seconds. Then pour them into a grinder jar. Grind at a high speed until you see a coarse powder of all the dry fruits.
2. Turn on the flame and pour ghee in the same pan over medium flame. Once the ghee is hot enough, transfer this powder into it along with the oats and poppy seeds. Sauté for a few minutes over medium heat until lumps start to form from the mixture.
3. After taking the mixture off the heat, keep it aside for cooling down. Then start making medium-sized balls from the mixture and store them in an air-tight container.

Makhana Kheer

A sweet dessert pudding or kheer usually made with *makhana* or foxnuts, milk, ghee, sugar and dry fruits. Lightweight and nutritious, foxnuts are also popular for being a very healthy snack.

INGREDIENTS

10 gms makhana
500 ml milk
10 pistachios
10 almonds
2 tsp stevia

METHOD

1. Pour milk in a saucepan and set it over medium-high heat. Once the milk comes to a boil, keep stirring so that the milk doesn't stick to the bottom of the pan.
2. After the milk has reduced by one-fourth of the volume, add the roasted makhana and continue cooking for the next 5 minutes.
3. Remove the kheer from the heat and add in the stevia and dry fruits, giving it a good mix. Also, make sure the stevia is completely dissolved.
4. Let the kheer cool down and serve it chilled.

Coconut Barfi

In Persian, barfi means snow and these coconut barfis are meant to look like snow. I inherited this recipe from my aunt, who prepares these without using any sugar – thus, making it a perfect addition to the book!

INGREDIENTS

100 gms mava
2 tbsp water
1 coconut (fresh), desiccated
4 tsp stevia
1 tsp cardamom powder
4–5 strands saffron
dry fruits for garnish as needed, chopped

METHOD

1. Pour the water in a pot and then add the mava, followed by stevia.
2. Add the desiccated coconut and gradually mix and roast until the coconut turns golden in colour.
3. Transfer to a greased pan now. Refrigerate for 3 hours and then cut into pieces. Garnish with saffron, chopped dry fruits and serve.

Fruit Kheer

This is an ideal dish for any celebratory occasion. You can get creative with this recipe by switching the fruits with the ones you prefer.

INGREDIENTS

1 small-sized orange
1 small-sized pomegranate
1 small-sized banana
1 small-sized apple
750 ml milk
2 tsp stevia

METHOD

1. In a saucepan set over medium heat, cook the milk, stirring it continuously until it has reduced to half the quantity. Keep an eye on it so the milk doesn't stick to the bottom of the pan.
2. Now, set the thickened milk off the heat and stir in the stevia.
3. Once the mixture reaches room temperature, store it inside the refrigerator.
4. In a bowl, chop the fruits into bite-sized pieces and add them to the thickened milk.
5. Serve the kheer chilled in another bowl.

Shrikhand

An easy-to-make, creamy yoghurt-based dessert from Maharashtrian cuisine, Shrikhand is often enjoyed as a dessert, but can also be served as a side dish to *pooris* or chapattis. And you can play around with numerous flavours, depending on your personal taste.

INGREDIENTS

3 cups yoghurt
2 tsp stevia
2 tbsp almonds, chopped
1 tbsp pistachios, chopped

METHOD

1. Take a cheesecloth and pour the yoghurt over it. Make sure a bowl is placed below to collect all the whey.
2. Squeeze the extra whey and place a weight over it.
3. Refrigerate for 1–2 hours.
4. Add stevia, followed by chopped almonds and pistachios.
5. Using a whisk or a spoon, stir the mixture until it is smooth in texture.
6. Now, serve it chilled and garnish it with some more chopped pistachios.

Sandesh

This delicacy is an import from Bengal, popular all over the country. With its rich, smooth texture, this sweet can satisfy your sweet cravings at any time. At least it does that for me!

INGREDIENTS

1 l full cream milk
2 lemons
½ **tsp** stevia
5 cardamom pods
20–25 **strands** saffron
12 pistachios

METHOD

1. In a heavy-bottomed vessel, simmer the milk on low heat.
2. In another bowl, add a little water to the lemon juice.
3. Bring the milk to a gentle boil. Then set it off the heat and, once the milk is lukewarm, add the lemon water to it slowly.
4. Keep stirring the mixture until the milk starts to coagulate into visible chhena.
5. Once the chhena has settled, strain it through a muslin cloth and pour some cold water over it. Then squeeze the cloth tightly to get rid of all the remaining water.
6. Transfer the chhena to another plate and keep kneading it into a dough for 5 to 6 minutes or until it reaches a smooth texture.
7. Add some cardamom powder and thinly chopped pistachios to the dough.
8. Now mix saffron and stevia into the chhena.
9. Once the dough is very smooth, roll into balls and flatten them slightly into a traditional *peda* shape until the entire mix is utilized .
10. Set it out in a plate and garnish with chopped pistachios pressed at the centre of the sweets.

Mava Cupcakes

Mava Cupcakes always trigger a bit of childhood nostalgia for me. It is their simplicity that makes them one of the most widely popular sweets among Indians.

INGREDIENTS

50 gms salted butter
10 gms stevia
150 gms yoghurt
105 gms all-purpose flour
1½ gms baking powder
½ gm baking soda
50 gms mava
2 gms cardamom

METHOD

1. Preheat the oven at 180°C. Line a 20x10 cm baking tin with parchment paper.
2. In a bowl, sift all the dry ingredients together: baking powder, baking soda, flour, stevia and cardamom.
3. In a separate bowl, blend together the yoghurt and butter.
4. Combine the dry and wet ingredients together to make a thick batter.
5. Pour the batter into individual silicone cupcake moulds on a tray till they are ¾ full. Tap the tray on the table to settle the batter.
6. Keep the tray in the preheated oven and bake for 30 minutes at 180°C.
7. Once the tray has cooled, demould, arrange them on a serving platter and serve with tea or coffee.

Rasgulla

These sweet spongy balls, similar to the rasmalai, originate from West Bengal and Odisha. In Bengal, the rasgulla is known as 'Banglar Rosogulla' and, in Odisha, they are known as 'Pahala Rasgulla'. They are also the right combination of a festive treat and an everyday delicacy, should you be craving non-oily, fresh sweets!

INGREDIENTS

1½ l milk
1–2 lemon
5–6 cardamom pods
1 tbsp stevia
1 l water

METHOD

1. In a heavy-bottomed vessel, add milk and let it simmer on low heat.
2. Add some water to the lemon juice.
3. Bring the milk to a gentle boil, turn off the heat and let the milk cool down. Now add lemon water to the slightly warm milk.
4. Keep stirring constantly. When the milk starts to coagulate, then stop adding milk.
5. Strain this mixture through a muslin cloth and pour some cold water over it. Hold the cloth tight and squeeze out every drop of water from it.
6. Once the chhena is ready, transfer it to another plate and start mashing it. Keep kneading for 5 to 6 minutes until smooth.
7. Start making small balls from the dough, ensuring they don't develop cracks on the sides.
8. Fill a nonstick pot with water and add stevia. Keep it on a medium-high flame to boil. Keep stirring it so that any lumps dissolve.
9. Once you can see the mixture boiling, start adding chhena balls one by one. Cover the pot for 7 to 10 minutes or until the chhena balls double in size.
10. Turn off the heat and refrigerate the rasgullas overnight.
11. Serve them chilled.

Rasmalai

The roots of rasmalai in India can be traced to West Bengal. These round sweets made from cottage cheese, or as it is colloquially known in Bengal, *chhana*, are soaked overnight in saffron and cardamom-flavoured milk, which give it a light and fluffy texture.

INGREDIENTS

- **1 l** milk
- **1–2** lemons
- **½ l** milk (for malai)
- **7–8 strands** saffron
- **8–10** pistachios
- **5–6** almonds
- **1 tsp** stevia

METHOD

1. In a heavy-bottomed vessel, set milk over low heat.
2. Add some water to the lemon juice. When you see the milk boiling gently, turn off the flame and let the milk cool down. Add lemon water to the milk in small increments.
3. Keep stirring constantly. When the milk starts to coagulate, stop adding the lemon water.
4. After straining through a muslin cloth, pour cold water over the mixture. Hold the cloth tightly and squeeze out all the water.
5. Transfer the resultant chhena to another plate and start mashing it. Keep kneading for 5 to 6 minutes until smooth.
6. Start making small balls without any cracks in them.
7. In a nonstick pot of water, add stevia and bring it to a boil over medium-high heat. Once the water starts vigorously boiling, start adding the chhena balls one by one. Cover the pot for 7 to 10 minutes or until the balls of chhena double in size.
8. Set the milk kept separately for malai over medium-high heat. Add stevia and saffron.
9. Keep stirring the milk to prevent it from sticking to the bottom of the saucepan. Once it has reduced by ¼ in quantity, turn off the heat.
10. Gently squeeze the chhena balls and drop them in saffron milk overnight.
11. Garnish with almonds and pistachios.

Gajar ka Halwa

We all pine for gajar ka halwa during the winters. One of the most beloved homemade desserts in India, it is primarily made with two simple ingredients: carrots and milk. I cannot stop myself from running to the kitchen whenever my mom makes gajar ka halwa and I've learned this recipe from her.

INGREDIENTS

1 kg carrots
1 l milk
2 tsp all-natural stevia
4 cardamom pods
10 strands kesar
20 almonds
10 pistachios

METHOD

1. Wash, peel and grate the carrots. Heat 2 teaspoons of ghee in a pan and then roast the carrots in it.
2. Add the milk to the pan and cook for 3–4 minutes until it comes to a boil. Then on a low flame, use a spatula to stir continuously.
3. Now add cardamom and continue to cook the halwa.
4. Add stevia when the milk is semi-absorbed. Continue cooking the halwa and make sure it doesn't stick to the bottom of the pan.
5. Keep stirring for 20–25 minutes at regular intervals.
6. Turn off the flame once the raw taste disappears. Decorate with almonds, pistachios and strands of saffron.

Besan Laddoo

Any festive season in India is incomplete without these iconic, melt-in-the-mouth golden-brown balls of gram flour. Although they may seem anathema for someone looking for sugar-free desserts, in this version, I can assure you they are fully worth the effort!

INGREDIENTS

2 cups besan (gram flour)
½ cup or **8–9 tbsp** ghee
2 tbsp stevia
1 tsp cardamom powder, optional
1 tbsp milk/water, optional

METHOD

1. In a metal pot, add the gram flour. Roast the gram on medium-low heat for 5 minutes or until the flour starts emanating a slightly nutty aroma. Make sure the flour doesn't stick to the bottom of the pot by stirring constantly.
2. Add ¾ of the ghee and continue stirring. As you are stirring, don't worry if you see lumps forming in the flour; keep stirring and they will go away eventually.
3. Slowly, the colour of besan will change to deep golden. Continue to roast for another 20 minutes or until you can sense a strong nutty aroma wafting from the pot.
4. Add the rest of the ghee to the gram flour and continue to cook on a low flame until you see ghee separating from the sides. At this stage, you should be able to see the gram flour forming a mass.
5. Turn off the flame and remove the besan mixture from the stove. Let it cool down now.
6. Add stevia and cardamom powder to the besan mixture and mix well.
7. Take a small portion of besan dough and start making round balls in the shape of laddoos.
8. Store them in an airtight container.

Shahi Falooda

The shahi falooda has all the essential elements: nuts, ice cream, milk and everything you can desire! This chilled drink-dessert is the perfect way to cool off in the summer heat.

INGREDIENTS

- **½ cup** vermicelli
- **2 tbsp** chia seeds
- **1½ cup** milk
- **1 tsp** stevia
- **5–10** saffron strands
- **2 tbsp** custard powder
- **2 tbsp** dry fruits
- **1 scoop** sugar-free vanilla ice cream

METHOD

1. Take a bowl, pour half a cup of milk into it, and add in the custard powder. Blend until you end up with a homogenous mixture without any lumps.
2. After adding a glass of milk to the custard mixture, boil it in a saucepan for 3–4 minutes.
3. Add a few saffron strands and all-natural stevia to it.
4. Don't let the mixture sit and make sure you mix it continuously. Turn off the flame and allow it to cool for 2–3 hours in the refrigerator after that.
5. In a pan, add a cup of water and vermicelli. Cook the vermicelli for 3–4 minutes until it becomes soft. Take it off the heat and wash under cold water. Strain the excess water and keep it aside.
6. In a bowl of water, add the chia seeds. Rest until the chia seeds have doubled in size.
7. Take a glass and add layers, starting with vermicelli, followed by a layer of custard and top it off with a mix of chia seeds.
8. You can add more vermicelli or soaked chia seeds, depending on your preference.
9. Add a scoop of vanilla ice cream and garnish it with some chopped nuts.

Videshi Desserts

Orange and Raspberry Galette
Dark Chocolate Brownies
Hazelnut Brownies
Strawberry Tea Cake
Mulberry Custard Tarts
Chocolate Popcorn
Strawberry Cheese Tarts
Ragi Chocolate Chip Cookies
Keto Almond Cookies
Ragi Mugcake
Oatmeal Cookies
Set Cheesecake
Apple Pie
Red Velvet Cupcakes
Chocolate Cupcakes
Meena's Banana Bread
Vanilla Chocolate Chip Muffins
Blueberry Muffins
Bounty Bars
Éclairs
Blueberry Ice Cream
Chocolate Strawberry Cake
Baked Hazelnut Cheesecake
Peanut Butter Cookies
Pancakes
Peanut Butter
Chocolate Ganache
Brookies
Granola Mix
Chocolate Mousse
Chocolate Bark
Crêpes
Chocolate Keto Spread

Orange and Raspberry Galette

This flaky, buttery, rustic French pastry is similar to tarts and pies. The shortcrust dough is rolled out and its centre is filled with fresh fruits and wrapped around the fruits. An ideal summer dessert, it does not need much fussing over to look and taste sumptuous!

INGREDIENTS

130 gms cold butter, cubed
30 gms stevia
225 gms all-purpose flour
50 ml milk
100 gms Greek yoghurt
1 orange
10–15 raspberries
5 gms stevia (for the yoghurt)
salt, to taste
black pepper, to taste

METHOD

1. In a bowl, rub in the cubed cold butter, flour and stevia together.
2. The mixture will have the texture of wet sand. Add milk and form a dough, but don't knead it.
3. Wrap the dough in cling wrap – even if it's not coming together as well as you want – and refrigerate for 3 hours.
4. Take out the dough from the fridge, flatten it by keeping the dough between two sheets of parchment paper with the help of a rolling pin.
5. The rolled sheet should be at least 15 cm in diameter and not thicker than 0.2 cm.
6. Preheat the oven to 180°C.
7. In another bowl, combine Greek yoghurt and stevia together.
8. Spread the yoghurt mixture in the centre, topping with deseeded orange slices and raspberries. Sprinkle salt and pepper over it.
9. Start folding from one corner and start overlapping each fold until all the sides are folded.
10. Glaze with milk and bake at 180°C for 1 hour.

Dark Chocolate Brownies

This classic brownie is my signature dish. They're rich, fudgy and easy to make, with a perfectly cracked top. And you'll never reach for the box mix again!

INGREDIENTS

200 gms sugar-free dark chocolate
100 gms butter
100 ml milk
80 gms all-purpose flour
80 gms ragi flour
1 tsp baking powder
1 banana
2 tbsp stevia

METHOD

1. Preheat the oven at 180°C. Line a 20x20 cm baking tin with parchment paper.
2. In a bowl, weigh out sugar-free dark chocolate and pour in lukewarm milk. Melt it over a double boiler or in the microwave and set it aside.
3. In another bowl, sift out the dry ingredients, i.e., ragi flour, stevia, refined flour and baking powder together.
4. Now combine the dry and wet ingredients into a uniform mixture.
5. Mash the banana separately with the help of a fork and fold it in.
6. Transfer the batter into the lined tray. Bake at 180°C for 25 to 30 minutes or until the skewer comes out clean.

Hazelnut Brownies

On days when I crave desserts, but don't wish to go out, this is one of my top choices to make at home.

INGREDIENTS

150 gms sugar-free dark chocolate
50 gms sugar-free hazelnut spread
100 gms butter
100 ml milk
80 gms all-purpose flour
80 gms ragi flour
2 tsp baking powder
20 gms flaxseeds
80 ml water
2 tbsp hazelnut spread (for garnish)
20 gms roasted hazelnut
2 tbsp stevia

METHOD

1. Preheat the oven at 180°C. Line a 20x20 cm baking tin with parchment paper.
2. In a small bowl, add both the flaxseeds and the water and set the bowl aside to soak for 10 minutes.
3. Add butter and chocolate in a bowl and melt them together.
4. Pour the milk into the chocolate mixture and mix it well.
5. Sift all-purpose flour, ragi flour and baking powder together in a separate bowl and set it aside.
6. Add the soaked flaxseeds to the chocolate mixture evenly.
7. Combine the dry and the wet ingredients together.
8. Pour the brownie batter into the lined tin.
9. Add 4 dollops of hazelnut spread and make random lines with help of a skewer. Also sprinkle roasted hazelnuts on top.
10. Bake at 180°C for 30 minutes or until the skewer comes out clean.

Strawberry Tea Cake

This tea cake is the perfect accompaniment to a cup of espresso or an evening snack while watching your favourite TV shows.

INGREDIENTS

160 gms all-purpose flour
16 gms brown rice flour
3 gms baking powder
2 gms baking soda
80 gms banana
170 gms curd
10 gms stevia
40 gms butter
100 ml water
14 strawberries

METHOD

1. Preheat the oven at 180°C.
2. Line a 20x20 cm baking tin with parchment paper.
3. In a bowl sift the all-purpose flour, rice flour, baking powder and baking soda together.
4. In a separate bowl blend banana, curd, stevia, butter and water together.
5. Combine the dry and wet ingredients together.
6. Pour the tea cake batter into a lined tin.
7. Chop strawberries one by two and place on top of the batter.
8. Bake at 180°C for 35 minutes or until the skewer comes out clean.

Mulberry Custard Tarts

As the winter season approaches, mulberries become available in the Indian bazaars. Because of their mild sweetness and sour taste, the berry compote pairs perfectly with the custard.

INGREDIENTS

130 gms cold butter, cubed
30 gms stevia
225 gms all-purpose flour
50 ml milk
40 gms custard powder
5 gms stevia
250 ml milk
15 gms butter
100 gms mulberry
100 ml water
½ tsp stevia (for the jam)
½ lemon

METHOD

Pastry

1. Preheat the oven at 180°C.
2. In a bowl, rub in the butter, flour and stevia together.
3. The mixture should have a sandy texture. Add the milk and roughly form a dough, but don't knead it.
4. Wrap it in cling wrap – even if it's not completely coming together – and refrigerate for 3 hours.
5. Roll out the chilled dough using a rolling pin between two sheets of parchment paper, about 0.2-cm thick.
6. Cut the sheets into round circles and line the tart ring with the tart dough.
7. Once the tarts are lined, freeze them for an hour.
8. Bake for 30 minutes at 180°C, or until the shells are golden in colour.

Custard

1. In a saucepan, weigh out half of the milk and stevia together.
2. Bring the milk to a boil in the saucepan.
3. In a bowl, pour the rest of milk, the custard powder, and combine them well.
4. Once the milk starts bubbling, pour the custard mixture into the saucepan.
5. Constantly keep whisking the custard until it thickens.

6. Turn off the heat and continue stirring. Mix in butter.
7. Empty the custard into a bowl and put on cling wrap touching the custard so that it doesn't form a skin. Let the custard cool at room temperature.

Mulberry Jam

1. Meanwhile, in a saucepan set over medium-high heat, start reducing mulberries, water, stevia and lemon juice.
2. Mash the berries until they turn into a purée with the help of a spatula.
3. Once mixture has completely reduced, turn off the flame.
4. Let the jam cool down completely.

Assembly

1. Pour the filling into the base of the cooled tart shell with mulberry jam.
2. Layer the jam with custard. Top it with mulberries.

Chocolate Popcorn

If you like caramel popcorn, you must give this recipe a try. These will satisfy all your sweet cravings from the comfort of your home without giving you a sugar rush either.

INGREDIENTS

20 gms popcorn
25 gms sugar-free chocolate
1 tsp salt
3 tsp coconut oil
2 tbsp cinnamon

METHOD

1. Preheat the oven at 165°C.
2. Cook one packet of instant popcorn and keep it aside.
3. Set chocolate and coconut oil over a double boiler. Once the mixture has melted, add salt and cinnamon.
4. Coat the popcorn with the chocolate sauce.
5. Empty the chocolate popcorn on a lined parchment tray. Bake at 165°C for 10 minutes and stir the mix every 2 minutes to avoid burning.
6. After it has cooled down, store the popcorn in an airtight container or enjoy immediately.

Strawberry Cheese Tarts

This tart screams Christmas when paired with cream cheese and a strawberry compote. It has got all the elements to make you feel like Christmas as soon as you look at it. The cream cheese mix is layered between tangy strawberry jam at the bottom and sweet fresh strawberry at the top and surrounded by a super crusty tart.

INGREDIENTS

130 gms cold butter, cubed
30 gms stevia
225 gms all-purpose flour
50 ml milk
100 gms strawberry
100 ml water
½ tsp stevia (for the jam)
½ lemon
150 gms cream cheese
10 gms stevia (for the cream cheese)
90 gms fresh cream

METHOD

Pastry

1. Preheat the oven at 180°C.
2. In a bowl, rub in the cubed butter and flour and stevia together.
3. It should look like wet sand. Once the mixture reaches this texture, pour in the milk and form a dough. Don't knead the dough.
4. Wrap the dough in a cling wrap even if it's not coming along together and store in the fridge for 3 hours.
5. Remove the dough from the fridge and flatten it between two sheets of parchment paper using a rolling pin, with a thickness of no more than 0.2 cm.
6. Cut the dough into rounds and line the tart rings with it.
7. Freeze the lined tart rings for an hour.
8. Bake at 180°C for 30 minutes or until they are golden in colour.

Strawberry Jam

1. In a saucepan, weigh out strawberry, water, stevia and lemon juice together.
2. Start reducing the mix in the saucepan over a medium-high flame.

3. Mash the strawberries into a purée with the help of a spatula.
4. Turn off the flame once mixture has completely reduced and set aside the jam to cool.

Cream Cheese Mix

1. In a bowl, soften the cream cheese, add fresh cream and stevia, and combine the mixture until it reaches a smooth texture.

Assembly

1. Fill the base of the tart with the jam.
2. Layer the jam with the cream cheese mix, with a couple of strawberries on top.

Ragi Chocolate Chip Cookies

The blend of ragi with delicious chocolates turns into a crumbly cookie that works just perfectly with a cup of tea or cappuccino after a long day or simply as a snack.

INGREDIENTS

105 gms all-purpose flour
100 gms ragi or flour millet
50 gms sugar-free chocolate, chopped
100 gms butter, melted
1 egg
30 gm stevia
1 tsp baking powder
1 tbsp gelatine powder
1 tsp vanilla extract

METHOD

1. Preheat the oven at 180°C.
2. In a bowl, sift together ragi flour and all-purpose flour. Add gelatin powder, baking powder and stevia.
3. To the dry ingredient mix, add melted butter, egg and vanilla extract.
4. Fold in chocolate chunks into the cookie dough.
5. Portion the dough into 30 gm each and place them on the lined baking sheet.
6. Bake the cookies at 180°C for 15 to 17 minutes or until the edges are golden brown.

Keto Almond Cookies

These almond cookies are tender on the outside and super soft on the inside. After baking, they look exactly like chocolate chip cookies.

INGREDIENTS

80 gms almond flour
1 tsp baking powder
2 tsp gelatine powder
50 gms sugar-free chocolate chips
50 gm butter
15 gm cream cheese
1 tsp vanilla extract
1 egg
2 tsp heavy cream

METHOD

1. Preheat the oven at 180°C.
2. In a bowl, melt the butter, cream cheese, vanilla extract and heavy cream together.
3. Add almond powder, gelatine powder and baking powder to the mix.
4. Combine the dry and the wet ingredients and add the egg to form a uniform mixture.
5. Fold in the chocolate chips into the batter.
6. Chill the batter for at least 4 hours or until it hardens.
7. Portion out the dough into cookie shapes.
8. Bake at 180°C for 20 minutes.

ADC

Ragi Mugcake

Do you crave a healthy dessert in the middle of the night at times? This delicious, healthy ragi mug cake is all you need to satisfy your midnight cravings.

INGREDIENTS

4 tbsp ragi flour
2 tbsp milk/plant-based milk (almond/oat milk)
2 tbsp cream
2 tsp all-natural stevia
¼ tbsp baking powder
2 tbsp cocoa powder
1 tbsp melted butter/ghee/ melted coconut oil
30 gms sugar-free dark chocolate, chopped/ chocolate chips
salt, a pinch

METHOD

1. In a mug, add the flour, cocoa powder, stevia, salt and baking powder. Stir or whisk to combine.
2. Add the oil or butter, non-dairy milk and vanilla into the mug with the dry ingredients and stir well with a spoon. Sprinkle the chocolate chips on top.
3. Cook in the microwave for 40 seconds. It will likely be a little undercooked in the middle at this point, which is how I enjoy it, but you can microwave it for another 10–20 seconds, if you prefer yours a little more baked.
4. Serve immediately.

Oatmeal Cookies

INGREDIENTS

3 tbsp flaxseed powder
9 tbsp water
2 over-ripe bananas
½ cup melted butter
1 tsp vanilla extract
2 tsp cinnamon
¼ tsp baking powder
½ tsp baking soda
¼ tsp salt
1¾ cup rolled oats flour
½ cup oats
1 cup raisins

METHOD

1. Preheat the oven at 180°C for 10 minutes.
2. In a bowl, soak flaxseed powder in water for 10 minutes.
3. In another large bowl, add mashed banana, cinnamon powder, baking powder, baking soda, butter, salt, vanilla extract and soaked flaxseeds.
4. Stir in the oats and the oats flour until the mix forms a dough.
5. Scoop the dough with an ice-cream scooper, place them on a lined tray and flatten the cookie dough.
6. Bake at 350°F/180°C for 15 minutes.

Set Cheesecake

The best thing about this light, creamy vanilla cheesecake is that it can be paired with any fruit of your choice.

INGREDIENTS

200 gms crackers
1 tsp stevia (for the base)
115 gms butter
300 ml sugar-free heavy/whipping cream
680 gms cream cheese
2 tbsp stevia (for the cream cheese)
60 gms fresh cream
2 tsp lemon juice
1 tsp vanilla extract

METHOD

1. Line a cheesecake tin with butter paper.
2. Grind the crackers into fine powder.
3. Add the melted butter and stevia to the powdered crackers.
4. Press down the crackers to the base of the cheesecake tin and freeze for an hour.
5. In a large bowl, whip the cream until it forms stiff peaks.
6. Soften the sour cream, lemon juice, stevia and cream cheese in a bowl.
7. Now fold the cream cheese mixture into the heavy/whipping cream.
8. Fill the cheesecake tin with cream cheese frosting and set it overnight in the fridge.

Apple Pie

This is a classic apple pie recipe with an irresistible homemade apple pie filling. From the best flaky pie crust to the generous saucy centre, this recipe comes out perfectly. If you love apples, this recipe is a must-try!

INGREDIENTS

130 gms cold butter, cubed
30 gms stevia
225 gms all-purpose flour
3 tbsp corn starch
1 tbsp cinnamon, ground
1 can unsweetened apple juice concentrate, thawed
6 cups apples, sliced

METHOD

1. Preheat the oven to 180°C.
2. In a bowl, mix the cubed butter, flour and stevia together.
3. Once the mixture reaches the texture of wet sand, add the milk and form a dough, but don't knead it.
4. Wrap in a cling wrap and refrigerate for 3 hours.
5. Flatten the dough between two sheets of parchment paper using a rolling pin, making sure the thickness is not more than 0.2 cm.
6. Cut the sheets into a round circle and line the pie ring with the tart dough.
7. Once the pie shell is lined, freeze it for an hour.
8. Wash, peel and finely slice the apples. Coat them with cinnamon and stevia.
9. In a pan, add butter and melt it. Now add the apples and cook them for 3 to 4 minutes over medium-high heat to make a compote.
10. Pour the apple compote in the lined pie tin and start covering the top with strips of tart dough to make a mat. Brush the pie with milk on top.
11. Bake at 180°C for 50 to 60 minutes or until the pie is golden brown in colour.

Optional

1. Whisk together corn starch, cinnamon and ⅓ cup of the apple juice

concentrate in a small bowl and set it aside.

2. In a large saucepan, simmer apples for about 10 minutes with the remaining concentrate until the apples become tender.
3. Pour the corn starch mixture into the saucepan and continue to simmer until the mix is thickened.
4. Remove from heat and spoon the apple mixture into a pastry-lined pie plate.
5. Cover with top crust. Seal and flute the edges, cutting steam vents on the top.
6. Bake at 180°C for 45 minutes, or until the crust looks golden brown.

Red Velvet Cupcakes

These iconic scarlet cupcakes are a perfect balance between vanilla and chocolate cupcakes. Topped with delicious vanilla cream cheese frosting, they will leave you wanting more.

INGREDIENTS

1 cup refined flour
1 cup ragi flour
1 tsp salt
1½ tbsp stevia
2 tsp baking soda
⅓ cup cocoa powder
½ cup melted butter
2 eggs
1 cup buttermilk
red food colour, a few drops

METHOD

1. Preheat your oven at 325°C.
2. In a mixing bowl, use a fork or whisk to mix together the flour, salt and baking soda. Then add the unsweetened cocoa powder.
3. Next, in a large mixing bowl, beat together the stevia and the oil.
4. Using a spatula, fold the dry ingredients into the mixing bowl. Do this by adding half of the dry ingredients at a time, working the batter in between to avoid lumps.
5. Add your eggs, one at a time, followed by buttermilk, food colouring, vanilla extract and vinegar. Do not over mix.
6. Once all the ingredients are smoothly combined, bake your cupcakes for 25–30 minutes or until a toothpick comes out clean. Allow them to cool fully before frosting.

Chocolate Cupcakes

If you love chocolates, this recipe may very well be your favourite in the present collection. Moist and full of chocolaty decadence, combined with the chocolate mousse frosting, it balances the sweetness with depth of flavour without giving you a migraine.

INGREDIENTS

150 gms sugar-free chocolate, melted
4 eggs
2 tbsp cocoa powder
2 cups almond flour
200 gms butter, melted
8 tbsp milk
2 tsp coffee
1 tsp baking powder
20 gms stevia
¼ tsp salt

METHOD

1. In a bowl, sift together almond flour, baking powder, coffee, stevia, salt and cocoa powder.
2. In a separate bowl, weigh out the milk, butter, melted chocolate and eggs.
3. Combine the dry and wet ingredients into a uniform mixture.
4. Pour the batter into lined cupcake moulds and bake them at 180°C for 20 to 55 minutes or until the skewers comes out clean.
5. Let the cupcakes cool down on a cooling rack and serve afterwards.

Meena's Banana Bread

If you love banana and chocolate, this recipe is a perfect union of both the ingredients. Plus, the addition of cinnamon is the proverbial cherry on top. This one is dedicated to my closest friend's mum, Meenakshi Aunty, who enjoys this banana bread and watches over us while resting in heaven.

INGREDIENTS

130 gms all-purpose flour
60 gms chocolate
3 bananas, ripe
2 gms baking powder
1 gm cinnamon powder
20 gm stevia
60 ml milk
100 gms butter
20 ml hot water
10 gms vanilla extract

METHOD

1. Preheat the oven to 180°C. Line a loaf tin with parchment paper.
2. In a bowl, melt butter and chocolate. Whisk the mixture and add warm milk and hot water to it.
3. In a separate bowl, mash the bananas. Fold in the vanilla extract and transfer the mix into the bowl with wet ingredients.
4. In a third bowl, sift flour. In the same bowl add baking powder and cinnamon powder.
5. Combine the dry and the wet ingredients together.
6. Pour the batter into the lined tin and bake at 180°C for 30 minutes.

Vanilla Chocolate Chip Muffins

Buttery and moist, the best part about this recipe is that the batter can be put together in less than 10 minutes as most of the ingredients are easily available in every home kitchen.

INGREDIENTS

120 gms flour, sifted
80 gms butter
130 ml milk
10 gms stevia
1 banana
50 gms sugar-free chocolate chips
2 gms baking soda
2 gms baking powder

METHOD

1. Preheat the oven at 180°C.
2. In a bowl, add the sifted flour, stevia, baking powder and baking soda.
3. Mash the banana separately and add milk and oil to the mix.
4. Gently combine the dry and wet ingredients.
5. Once the batter is almost combined, fold in the chocolate chips.
6. Line a cupcake pan.
7. Pour the batter into the lined cupcake moulds and bake for 25 minutes at 180°C..

Blueberry Muffins

These blueberry muffins are really easy to make and come out with a moist and tender centre, bursting with blueberries and a golden-brown top.

INGREDIENTS

120 gms butter
1 cup stevia
2 eggs
2 cups all-purpose flour
½ tsp salt
2 tsp baking powder
1 cup almond milk
2 tbsp blueberry compote (without sugar)

METHOD

1. Preheat the oven at 375°C. Line a muffin tray.
2. In a mixing bowl, cream together your butter, stevia and eggs.
3. In a smaller bowl, mix together the dry ingredients: flour, salt and baking powder.
4. Slowly add the dry ingredients to the first mixing bowl.
5. Fold in the vanilla extract and almond milk.
6. Remove the bowl from the mixer and by hand, gently fold in the blueberries. Do not over mix as this will break up the blueberries.
7. Fill about two-thirds of each muffin cup. Pour some of the blueberry compote over the lined muffins. Use a toothpick to spread it into a swirl. Bake for 25 to 30 minutes. Let it cool before serving.

Bounty Bars

This recipe is chock-full of nostalgia as well as decadence. These chocolate bars are inspired by the eponymous candies – a childhood favourite. Wholesome and filled with desiccated coconut, they are coated with high-quality cooking chocolate all over.

INGREDIENTS

200 gms sugar-free dark chocolate
1 tsp stevia
60 gms coconut, desiccated
150 ml milk
15 gms ghee

METHOD

1. In a pan, heat ghee.
2. Add the desiccated coconut to the ghee and roast them for 3 to 5 minutes until the mix is light golden in colour.
3. Pour the milk into the pan and add stevia to it.
4. Cook until the milk has evaporated, and you are left with a sticky coconut mixture.
5. Quickly empty the content of the pan onto a lined parchment tray and flatten the coconut mixture until you get a mass 2–3 cm in height.
6. Cut the flattened coconut mixture into rectangles of 7x3 cm. You should be able to get around five. Keep inside the freezer for 30 minutes.
7. Melt the sugar-free dark chocolate in a double boiler or in the microwave.
8. Dunk the coconut rectangle in the melted chocolate using a fork and drizzle out the excess chocolate. Place it back on the parchment paper. Continue the process for rest of the rectangles.
9. Chill the bars in the fridge for enjoying them later.

Éclairs

Éclairs are logs of choux pastry with big air pockets, which makes it easy to fill with a cream of your choice. These are buttery and melt-in-the-mouth French desserts that you simply cannot resist and, in this version, are made with absolutely no sugar.

INGREDIENTS

50 gms butter
125 gms milk
5 gms stevia
½ tsp vanilla
75 gms all-purpose flour
2 eggs
1 cup sugar-free heavy/whipping cream

METHOD

1. Preheat the oven at 210°C.
2. In a saucepan, weigh out the butter, milk, stevia and vanilla extract.
3. Place the pan over medium-high flame and bring the mixture to a boil. Whisk the mixture until bubbles start vigorously forming on the surface.
4. Empty the flour into the milk mixture and continue stirring. You might notice some clumps in the mixture by now, so use a spatula to keep working the batter.
5. Keep stirring. Eventually, it will leave the sides of the pan.
6. Cook for 5 minutes until you see a dough forming in the pan as you keep stirring.
7. Turn off the heat and transfer the dough into a bowl. Let it cool down completely.
8. Once it has cooled down, start adding one egg at a time. Combine the batter with the help of a spatula.
9. Using a piping bag with a round nozzle, and fill the bag with the choux pastry batter.
10. Line a tray with parchment paper and pipe a 7- cm straight line of éclair. Do this for the rest of the batter.

11. Freeze the piped éclairs for an hour.
12. Bake for 20 to 25 minutes at 210°C until they are golden in colour. Do not open the oven.
13. Reduce the temperature to 150°C and continue to bake for another 40 minutes until they are golden brown in colour.
14. Remove from the oven and let the éclairs cool down.
15. Cut the éclairs from the centre and fill the base with sugar-free whipped cream.
16. Dunk the top of the éclairs in melted chocolate.

Blueberry Ice Cream

You can now make picturesque purple ice cream without any food colouring or an ice cream churner at home and it is creamier than your store-bought ice cream. Since there are no additives in this recipe, enjoy the ice cream as soon as it comes out of the freezer as it will start melting otherwise.

INGREDIENTS

100 gms blueberries
20 gms stevia
1 whole egg
1 egg yolk
115 gms sugar-free heavy/whipping cream

METHOD

1. In saucepan, add blueberries and place the pan over medium heat. Start cooking for 5 to 7 minutes or until the blueberries look completely mashed. Then turn off the heat and set the pan aside.
2. In a bowl, break the whole egg and whisk it with the separated egg yolk until the volume has doubled.
3. Fill a saucepan with water for double boiling. Once the water comes to a boil, place the bowl of eggs in it and keep whisking to prevent the eggs from curdling. Keep whisking until the mix turns pale in colour. This will take around 7 to 10 minutes.
4. Then add the blueberry paste into the whisked eggs and cook over the double boiler for another 5 minutes.
5. Add stevia to the blueberry mixture off the heat, making sure the stevia is completely dissolved.
6. In a bowl, gently fold in the blueberry mixture and heavy/whipping cream.
7. In a lined tin, pour the ice cream batter and freeze for 5 to 8 hours.
8. Scoop and serve.

Chocolate Strawberry Cake

Chocolate strawberry cake is the easiest layered chocolate cake to make. All you need are fresh strawberries, chocolate ganache and a decadent chocolate sponge.

INGREDIENTS

150 gm all-purpose flour
100 ml oil
180 ml milk
150 gms sugar-free chocolate, chopped
30 gms cocoa powder
70 gms fresh cream
3 eggs
50 gms stevia
1 tsp baking soda
1 tsp baking powder
strawberries, as required

METHOD

Chocolate Sponge

1. Preheat the oven at 180°C.
2. Line a 20x20 cm baking tin with parchment paper.
3. In a bowl sift together flour, baking powder, baking soda, stevia and cocoa powder.
4. In a separate bowl, weigh out milk, oil and eggs.
5. Combine the dry and wet ingredients into a uniform mixture.
6. Bake at 180°C for 40 to 45 minutes.
7. Let the cake cool down on a cooling rack.
8. Trim the edges of the sponge and divide into three separate layers.

Cake Syrup

1. In a saucepan, set the water and stevia over medium-high heat.
2. Cook until it reaches the first boil.
3. Let it cool down.

Chocolate Ganache

1. In a saucepan, bring cream to a boil and keep stirring it.
2. Pour the hot cream over the chopped chocolate in a bowl and mix constantly until the chocolate dissolves.

3. Once the mixture is rested and looks stiff enough to pipe, transfer the ganache into a piping bag with the desired nozzle.

Assembly

1. Place one layer of the sponge on the cake board and soak it with cake syrup. Now spread ganache on top of it.
2. Repeat this for the other two layers.
3. Coat the side of the cake with ganache.
4. To decorate, pipe the dollops on top of the cake, tucking strawberries in between each of them.

Baked Hazelnut Cheesecake

This authentic New York-style cheesecake is super creamy. The best part about it is that it's made with very few ingredients and is completely sugar-free.

INGREDIENTS

100 gms digestive biscuits (sugar-free)
30 gms butter
335 gms cream cheese
70 gms fresh cream
10 gms stevia
2 eggs
70 gms hazelnut spread

METHOD

1. Preheat the oven at 180°C and line a 6-inch baking tin with parchment paper.
2. In a mixer, grind the biscuits to a complete powder.
3. Add melted butter to the biscuit powder.
4. Flatten the base on a lined baking tin.
5. Bake in the oven for 5 minutes at 180°C.
6. Let it completely cool down.

Batter

1. In a bowl, weigh the cream cheese and soften it with a hand beater.
2. Once smoothened, add fresh cream and stevia and keep mixing until it is uniformly combined.
3. Add one egg at a time and whisk until the mixture is uniform.
4. Pour the batter onto the biscuit base.
5. Place a hot-water bath tray on the lower rack of the oven and bake the cheesecake on the middle rack for 50 minutes at 180°C or until the centre is slightly jiggly.
6. Spread the hazelnut chocolate spread using a spoon, and add some chopped roasted hazelnuts on top.

Peanut Butter Cookies

These classic peanut butter cookies are a crowd pleaser. They are delicate and have a velvety texture, immediately melting in the mouth.

INGREDIENTS

85 gms butter, room temperature
10 gms stevia
105 gms all-purpose flour
2 gms baking powder
45 gms peanut butter

METHOD

1. Preheat the oven at 180°C.
2. In a bowl, combine peanut butter, butter, stevia, flour, baking powder together until they form a soft dough.
3. Chill the dough until it hardens.
4. Portion into 25-gm portions and place them on a parchment paper.
5. Bake at 180°C for 12 to 15 minutes.

Pancakes

This classic breakfast dish can be topped with cream, fruits and chocolates to make it an even more decadent treat for your morning meal.

INGREDIENTS

180 gms all-purpose flour
30 gms butter, melted
200 ml milk
2 eggs
10 gms stevia
2 gms baking powder
2 gms baking soda

METHOD

1. In a large bowl, mix the flour, stevia, baking soda and baking powder.
2. In another bowl, mix the milk, eggs and melted butter.
3. Combine the dry and wet ingredients to form a thick batter.
4. Place a nonstick pan over medium-high heat and grease with butter.
5. Start by adding one ladle of pancake batter. Wait for the top to bubble before flipping the pancake to the other side and cook until they are golden brown in colour.
6. Repeat the process for the rest of the batter.

Peanut Butter

A breakfast scoop, a lunchbox spread over a slice of bread, a pre-work out or just a dollop on your Asian noodle bowl, this one can be used in innumerable ways to make your dishes tasty.

INGREDIENTS

1 cup unsalted roasted peanuts
1 tbsp coconut oil
1 tsp stevia (optional)

METHOD

1. Add warm peanuts to a food processor or pulse for 5 seconds to break down the peanuts.
2. Process at high speed for 1 minute until the peanut mixture looks like wet sand. Scrape down the sides and bottom of the bowl.
3. Continue at high speed for 1 minute. The peanuts will start to clump together and form a mass. Scrape down the sides and the bottom of the bowl.
4. Process again at high speed for 1 minute. The peanuts should become smooth by now. Add coconut oil and blitz until it looks like thick peanut butter. Scrape down the sides and the bottom of the bowl or cup again.
5. Add stevia and mix at high speed for 1 to 2 minutes until the peanut butter is smooth and can be poured. Once the peanut butter cools, it thickens and can be spread easily.
6. Transfer the warm peanut butter to a jar or airtight container.

Chocolate Ganache

Chocolate ganache can be used as a filling, spread, dip, topping, frosting. It is also one of the easiest preparations listed in this book.

INGREDIENTS

100 gm sugar-free chocolate, chopped
200 ml heavy/fresh cream

METHOD

1. In a saucepan, bring cream to a boil and keep stirring it.
2. In a bowl, pour the hot cream over the chopped chocolates and mix constantly until chocolate dissolves. Set it aside for resting.
3. Once the ganache is stiff enough to pipe, fill it in a piping bag with the desired nozzle to use in your dishes.

Brookies

On the days when you can't choose whether you want to eat a brownie or a cookie, this will be your go-to recipe. Brookies are the perfect middle ground for cookie and brownie lovers – extremely chocolatey, fudgy and cakey at the same time.

INGREDIENTS

225 gms sugar-free chocolate
65 gms butter
2 eggs
15 gms stevia
115 gms all-purpose flour
10 gms baking powder
salt, a pinch

METHOD

1. Preheat the oven at 180°C.
2. Line a baking tray with parchment paper.
3. Break eggs in a big bowl and beat them with the help of a hand beater until light and fluffy or they triple in quantity.
4. Melt the sugar-free chocolate and butter in a separate bowl.
5. Sift flour, baking powder, salt and stevia together.
6. Delicately combine the chocolate mixture into eggs in three parts, making sure the eggs don't settle down.
7. Fold in the flour into wet ingredients in three parts and avoid over-mixing them.
8. Chill the dough for 4 hours or until it hardens.
9. Portion the dough in 40-g pieces and place them on the baking tray lined with parchment paper.
10. Once they reach room temperature, bake them at 180°C for 15 minutes.

Granola Mix

This easy-to-make granola recipe uses nine ingredients easily available at home.

INGREDIENTS

200 gms rolled oats
40 gms cashews
40 gms almonds
40 gms seeds
5 gms pink salt
10 gms cocoa powder
60 gms sugar-free chocolate
30 ml coconut oil
10 gms stevia

METHOD

1. Preheat the oven to 180°C.
2. In a baking tray, roast the almond, cashew nut and seeds for 3 to 4 minutes.
3. In a separate bowl, melt chocolate and coconut oil together and set it aside.
4. Combine the rolled oats, cashews, almonds seeds, salt, stevia and cocoa powder, with the wet ingredients.
5. Bake for 10 to 12 minutes at 180°C in a baking tray.
6. Once it reaches room temperature, store the mix in an airtight container.

Chocolate Mousse

This is a classic chocolate mousse prepared using the traditional French method. It uses less cream and more chocolate, creating a more intense chocolate flavour and a beautiful creamy texture.

INGREDIENTS

50 gms sugar-free dark chocolate
15 gms salted butter
15 ml coconut oil (optionally, instead of butter)
1 tbsp cocoa powder
200 ml coconut cream
1 tbsp stevia
cinnamon powder, as needed

METHOD

1. Melt the chocolate and butter together. If doing this in a microwave, heat for about 30 seconds.
2. Whip together cream, cocoa powder and stevia, and add to the chocolate and butter mix.
3. Slowly add the cinnamon powder.
4. Whip until soft peaks are formed and transfer to a bowl.
5. Top with berries and mint leaves, if you wish.
6. Refrigerate for at least an hour and serve cold.

Chocolate Bark

This recipe for a rich, lush chocolate bark is one of the simplest candy recipes for baking beginners.

INGREDIENTS

200 gm sugar-free dark chocolate
20 gm almond, sliced
20 gm pistachios, sliced
2 tbsp rose petals
seeds and other nuts, optional

METHOD

1. Line a baking tray with parchment paper.
2. Melt chocolate in a bowl.
3. Empty the chocolate on a lined tray and spread it with the help of an off-set knife. Make sure the chocolate does not start melting in your hand.
4. Once the chocolate is evenly spread, sprinkle the pistachios, almonds and rose petals on top of it.
5. Let the chocolate set at room temperature for around 10 to 15 minutes.
6. Once the bark is set, break it into your desired size and shape.
7. Store in an airtight container.

Crêpes

These delicate homemade crêpes with buttery crisp edges will make for an amazing and quick breakfast meal.

INGREDIENTS

100 gms all-purpose flour
220 gms milk
2 eggs
10 gms stevia
20 gms butter

METHOD

1. In a large bowl, mix flour, stevia, baking soda and baking powder.
2. In a separate bowl, whisk together milk, eggs and melted butter.
3. Combine the dry and wet ingredients to form a thick batter.
4. Place a nonstick pan over medium-high heat and grease with butter.
5. Start by adding one ladle of crêpe batter, spread it evenly on the pan. Wait for the top to dry, flip the crêpe to the other side and cook until it is golden in colour. Flip the crêpe again and cook for another minute.
6. Repeat the process with the rest of the batter.

Chocolate Keto Spread

All you need for this recipe is a powerful mixer grinder. And you can balance the flavour of the nuts according to your preference.

INGREDIENTS

½ cup sugar-free dark chocolate, chopped into small pieces
1 cup roasted peanuts
⅙ cup cocoa powder
1 cup roasted hazelnuts
1 tsp stevia
pink salt, a pinch

METHOD

1. Grind the peanuts, cocoa powder, hazelnuts, stevia and chopped chocolates into a paste.
2. If it starts to break down into clumps, scrape down the sides and start grinding again until it becomes a smooth paste.
3. Store in an airtight container at room temperature.

A
DIABETIC
CHEF

Smoothies and Bowls

Super Smoothie
Strawberry Cream Bowl
Green Smoothie
Breakfast Smoothie
Chia Seed Pudding
Parfait

Super Smoothie

When you are on the go and don't have time to cook something heavy and nutritious, this recipe will be your lifesaver. It's extremely flavourful, made with blueberries and Greek yoghurt. Just blend all the ingredients and your smoothie is ready.

INGREDIENTS

Smoothie

1 cup blueberries, frozen
1 banana, frozen
½ cup coconut milk
½ cup Greek yoghurt
½ cup oats

Toppings

1 tbsp pumpkin seeds
1 tbsp chia seeds
1 tbsp coconut flakes
1 tsp stevia
2 pcs hazelnut bar
10 pcs almonds
peanut butter, as needed
almond butter, as needed

METHOD

1. Blend the smoothie ingredients on low power until only small bits are visible.
2. Add some of the coconut or Greek yoghurt – based on your preference – and blend on low again, scraping down the sides as needed, until the mixture reaches a soft-serve consistency.
3. Serve it in a bowl – and finish with your favourite toppings.

Note:

You can add 2 cups of baby spinach to make the smoothie healthier. Or blend rolled or crushed oats to give the smoothie a thicker consistency. Chia seeds can also be added for a similar effect.

Around 3–4 ice cubes can be added to make the smoothie cool and frothy and give it the consistency of a sorbet.

A dollop of peanut or almond or hazelnut butter can be alternatively added to make the smoothie richer and creamier. If you are not planning to immediately consume it, it can be refrigerated and consumed for up to 2 days.

Strawberry Cream Bowl

Topped with strawberries, granola and desiccated coconut, this yummy bowl is as heavenly to look at as it is to eat.

INGREDIENTS

10 strawberries, frozen
½ cup Greek yoghurt
¼ cup almond milk
1 tsp stevia
¼ tsp vanilla
½ cup granola
5 strawberries
8 blueberries
2 tbsp almonds
1 tbsp pumpkin seeds
1 tsp chia seeds

METHOD

1. Blend the strawberries, yoghurt, maple syrup and vanilla until it reaches a smooth consistency.
2. Transfer to a bowl and top with the granola, strawberries, blueberries, almonds, pumpkin seeds and chia seeds.

Green Smoothie

Green smoothies are a simple conduit to incorporate vitamins and minerals into your diet. This recipe offers both taste and nutrition.

INGREDIENTS

1 cup spinach
1 banana, frozen
½ cup almond milk
1 tsp stevia
½ cup Greek yoghurt
½ cup coconut water

METHOD

1. Make sure your blender is powerful enough to blend frozen fruit.
2. Add all ingredients in the order listed here. Blend on high for at least 2 minutes or until you see a smooth texture. Scrape down the sides of the blender as needed. The smoothie will be very thick.
3. Pour into a bowl and add toppings. Store any leftover smoothie in a box with a lid in the refrigerator for up to 8–10 hours.

Breakfast Smoothie

This is another quick recipe for a healthy, filling meal to start your day.

INGREDIENTS

½ cup cauliflower
1 cup banana, frozen
½ cup almond milk
10 blueberries
½ tsp stevia
granola mix, optional
freeze-dried banana, optional
blueberries, optional
mint leaves, optional
edible flowers, optional

METHOD

1. Combine all of the ingredients in a blender.
2. Blend until smooth.
3. Garnish with granola mix, or a freeze-dried banana or berries of your choice (I prefer blueberries) along with some sprigs of mint and edible flowers.

Chia Seed Pudding

You can serve this pudding as a breakfast pudding or have it as a healthy snack. Topped with strawberry and blueberry or any berry of your choice, it's not only wholesome but also very tasty.

INGREDIENTS

100 gms chia seeds
30 gms fresh cream
½ tsp stevia
5 strawberries
5 blueberries

METHOD

1. Soak the chia seeds in the water overnight.
2. Mix the cream, chia seeds and stevia together and layer in a bowl.
3. Top it with berries of your choice.

Parfait

This light, layered dessert can be both served for brunch or enjoyed as a snack.

INGREDIENTS

½ cup Greek yoghurt
½ cup strawberries
½ cup blueberries
½ cup granola
½ tsp stevia

METHOD

1. Combine the Greek yoghurt and stevia.
2. Add layers of Greek yoghurt and top with granola.
3. Layer the granola with blueberries and strawberries.
4. Repeat steps 1 and 2 again.

Beverages

Caffè Mocha
Lemon Iced Tea
Cinnamon Hot Chocolate
Ginger Lemonade
Avocadoade
Pomegranate Spritzer
Masala Chai
Strawberry Milkshake

Caffè Mocha

It comes as no surprise that the richness of Belgian dark chocolate with the strong aroma of coffee make for a heavenly combination for people who enjoy both flavours.

INGREDIENTS

1 glass skimmed milk
½ tbsp cocoa powder
½ tbsp instant coffee
1 tsp stevia
½ tsp vanilla extract
20 gm 55 per cent dark chocolate

METHOD

1. In a pan, boil the milk.
2. Add cocoa powder, instant coffee powder, all-natural stevia and vanilla extract to the boiling milk.
3. Mix it consistently until there are no lumps left.
4. Melt the dark chocolate on a double boiler, ensuring a smooth consistency for the chocolate.
5. Pour the chocolate into the hot coffee mix and stir until it becomes a homogeneous mixture.

Lemon Iced Tea

One of the most refreshing summertime treats is a tall glass of iced tea. Readymade iced tea, although handy, is neither as refreshing nor as tasty as this one, freshly brewed at home.

INGREDIENTS

2 tbsp black tea powder
2 glasses water
1 lemon
2 tsp stevia
10 (approx.) ice cubes
2 lemon wheels
mint leaves, optional

METHOD

1. In a medium-sized saucepan, add 2 glasses of water, black tea powder and all-natural stevia.
2. Boil it until you start seeing bubbles and allow it to simmer for a couple of minutes.
3. Turn off the flame and squeeze in the lemon juice while simultaneously stirring it.
4. Allow the tea mixture to cool off.
5. Once your lemon tea has reached room temperature, you can serve it with some ice cubes or refrigerate it overnight.
6. Your lemon iced tea is ready, and you can serve it with fresh mint leaves and a lemon wheel!

Cinnamon Hot Chocolate

On a cold winter day, there is nothing more perfect than a cup of warm and delicious homemade hot chocolate with cinnamon.

INGREDIENTS

1½ cup milk
100 gms sugar-free dark chocolate
½ tsp stevia
2 tbsp cocoa powder
sea salt, a pinch
1 tbsp sugar-free whipped coconut cream
1 cinnamon stick

METHOD

1. In a saucepan, heat the milk over medium flame.
2. Add cocoa powder to boiling milk and then blend in the stevia.
3. Once the mixture starts bubbling, keep stirring to prevent any lumps.
4. Break the dark chocolate into blocks and add to the milk until it becomes thick and boils well. Lower the flame once mixed.
5. Now that the hot chocolate is ready, pour it in a serving cup or glass. Cover the top with a small blob of coconut cream. Use a cinnamon stick to stir and then rest it for a minute. Sip it while it's hot.

Ginger Lemonade

There's no better drink to cool off with on a summer day than a refreshing glass of ginger lemonade. The strong spicy flavour of ginger works wonderfully with the tanginess of lemon. And, of course, in our version, though we make it without adding sugar, it is sweet enough for you to enjoy as a refreshing beverage.

INGREDIENTS

1 glass water
1 lemon
1 tsp stevia
5 ml ginger juice
2–3 sprigs mint leaves
3–4 ice cubes

METHOD

1. Take a bowl/jug and add a glass of chilled water.
2. Squeeze the lemon into it.
3. Add a teaspoon of stevia to it.
4. Mix this well with a ladle.
5. Add some mint leaves to it.
6. Stir in ginger juice.
7. Serving Suggestions: Add some crushed ice in a glass and pour your lemonade into it. Garnish it with some mint leaves and a slice of lemon.

Avocadoade

It is the combination of avocado and cucumber that makes this fresh drink special. Often consumed as a detox drink, it actually works much better than all other such potions you might have come across.

INGREDIENTS

1 wedge avocado
1⅓ cup cucumber juice
⅓ cup aloe vera juice
⅓ cup lemon juice
1 tsp stevia
2 cucumber wheels

METHOD

1. In a food processor, blend an avocado wedge with some cucumber juice.
2. Add some ice cubes and a tablespoon of all-natural stevia.
3. Add ⅓ cup of aloe vera juice and ⅓ cup of lemon juice.
4. Blend again until it reaches a smooth texture.
5. Serve chilled. Pour some of it in a glass filled with crushed ice or top it with a cucumber wheel.

Pomegranate Spritzer

This fizzy drink is fun and easy to make. When you are running out of time, it's the quickest drink to put together, using a simple combination of pomegranate and soda.

INGREDIENTS

60 ml pomegranate juice
400 ml soda
½ tsp stevia
2 tbsp pomegranate seeds

METHOD

1. In a glass, add pomegranate juice and stevia.
2. Add soda.
3. Top with pomegranate seeds.

Masala Chai

This hot beverage is an essential element of everyday lives in India. This recipe allows anyone who cannot have sugar to also enjoy their daily chais!

INGREDIENTS

2 tbsp black tea powder
1 glass water
1 glass milk
2 tsp stevia
5 black peppercorns
2 cardamom pods

METHOD

1. In a saucepan, add milk, water, black tea powder, black pepper and cardamom and place it over a high flame and bring to a boil.
2. Boil the tea until dark brown in colour and strain the tea in a kettle.
3. Serve in a teacup and consume it hot.

Strawberry Milkshake

This is an old-school American dream drink. It is topped with sugar-free whipped cream, making it guilt-free for your consumption.

INGREDIENTS

10–12 strawberries, frozen
250 ml milk
1 tsp stevia
50 ml fresh cream
50 gms sugar-free whipped cream
5–6 ice cubes

METHOD

1. In a food processor, blend the strawberries until you see a smooth paste.
2. Blend in milk, fresh cream and stevia.
3. Add some ice and pour the shake into a glass.
4. Garnish with some freshly chopped strawberries and top with a dollop of whipped cream.

A Note from the Chef

I have been cooking since I was in the third grade and got diagnosed with diabetes. With the diagnosis came the restrictions of not being able to eat a lot of things I loved. I made a promise to myself that I would attempt to ensure every diabetic person is able to enjoy their favourite sweets, in whatever capacity or quantity. This book is a culmination of seven years of work, developing recipes and learning in the course of conversations with doctors, nutritionists and food scientists.
It contains a myriad range of sweets – both Indian and from around the globe, customized for people like me who manage diabetes on a daily basis.

Usually, diabetes can be managed through a combination of exercise, healthcare and dietary planning.
If you are able to ensure you are doing the first two, this book has got the last part covered. It has everything – from brownies to cinnamon hot chocolate, falooda to fruit kheer. Most of these can be prepared in around half an hour, and with ingredients that are commonly found in our houses. This is an attempt to get rid of the dogmatic view that diabetics cannot have desserts. If you are diabetic, and love your desserts, all you need to do is know is a few clever culinary techniques and carefully curated ingredients. I thoroughly enjoyed writing this book, and I hope you enjoy making and eating the dishes in it because who says diabetics can't eat desserts?

Acknowledgements

I want to dedicate this book to my father and mother, who have always stayed by my side – through my childhood to the person I am today.

Needless to say, I want to thank my close friend Preeti Deshmukh, who has been my mentor and support system throughout the journey of the book as I learned more about nutrition and food every day.

My special thanks to Insiya Mithaiwala from my kitchen team – for her constant efforts and engagement in the process of completing this book. I also need to thank Tanya, Rohin, Darshit, Mohit, Dhruv and all my team members and friends who helped us through the steps.

I must express my gratitude to Alok Verma, an immensely talented photographer, who was extraordinarily supportive throughout our journey of creating this book.

Finally, my thanks to the entire team at Pan Macmillan India for helping me put together the book: my editor Isha Banerji, without whose help, we wouldn't be able to achieve half as much of what we did, Haitenlo Semy, who designed the book and the cover, and Sohini Biswas, who proofread it.

Conversion Table

ALL-PURPOSE FLOUR

1 cup	120 gms
½ cup	60 gms
¼ cup	30 gms

BUTTER

1 cup	220 gms
½ cup	110 gms
¼ cup	55 gms

LIQUID

1 cup	200 gms
½ cup	100 gms
¼ cup	50 gms

OVERALL

1 cup	16 tbsp
¾ cup	12 tbsp
½ cup	8 tbsp
¼ cup	4 tbsp